STRETCH YOUR THINKING

HOW TO THINK LIKE

Will Smith

This is "How to think like Will Smith". Now, this book is written by Lance Coleman. It is also performed by Lance Coleman. Recorded at Lance Coleman's house, and engineered, mixed and mastered by Lance Coleman. But this book is about Will Smith. I'd been really inspired by a lot of great people, some of them famous, some of them not. They've all been great thinkers that caused me to stretch my own thinking and how I approach the world around me.

This series will serve as an homage to these people. Hopefully, I can share what I've learned, from what I know about these people, what I've read, what I've heard in rumors, in stories, what I've seen in front of me in movies, books, interviews. And I'm going to filter out the information that you need. I'm going to filter out the most impactful and insightful aspects of their life because these were impactful on my life. And hopefully, they can have the same kind of upliftment and widening in yours, as well.

WILL SMITH IS
ONE OF THE
MOST ENIGMATIC
PEOPLE IN THE
WORLD. AND
HERE, WHAT
ENIGMATIC
MEANS, IS
WILL SMITH
LIKE

WHY WILL?

If you look anywhere in the culture, currently you'd be hard pressed to find an aspect of it that he hasn't participated in. I mean, he's one of the most powerful actors in Hollywood, while at the same time being one of the most accepted and primitive hip-hop artists that have ever lived.

His youthful nature and his ability to stay on The Cutting Edge of what it even means to be a human being, has made him one of the most attractive personalities that have ever graced the screen, or track, or script, or production. These are just to list a few of the achievements he's had.

WILL SMITH HAS ACCOMPLISHED NOT ONLY EVERYTHING WE COULD EXPECT FROM HIM, BUT EVEN THINGS WE DIDN'T EXPECT FROM HIM.

Listed as Forbes' One of the Most Bankable Stars almost every year, he has films that had leading roles and accumulated over 100 million dollars. Five of them hit 500 million dollars. He has a net worth of hundreds of millions, we all know who his wife is, his kids are famous in their own right and not only famous, but famous for the right reasons.

By all accounts, Will Smith has accomplished not only everything we could expect from him, but even things we didn't expect from him. Because of that, I've grown a deep and great appreciation for what he contributes to the world. And, more importantly, for me personally, the image of a black man in America.

99% OF PEOPLE ARE NOT WILLING TO DO WHAT IT TAKES TO MAKE THEIR DREAMS COME TRUE.

- WILL SMITH

ON THIS PAGE, WRITE DOWN EVERYTHING HOLDING YOU BACK. THEN CROSS THEM OUT. THERE'S NOTHING THAT CAN HOLD YOU BACK.

ACTIVITY

CHANGE

One of the things that was really impactful and that's always stated about his lifestyle, is that he really focuses on the fact that 99% of people are not willing to do what it takes to make their dreams come true

And I think he meant to say that not in a discouraging way, but more in a way that people with aspirations, no matter how deeply they want to do it, don't always want to take the steps to do it. And more importantly, they don't want to change themselves, to accomplish the things that they need.

THEY DON'T WANT TO CHANGE THE ASPECTS OF THEMSELVES THAT HAVE TO CHANGE, TO GET TO THE BIGGER PICTURE.

Will Smith says that the center of bringing any dream into fruition, is not necessarily this radical thought, but it is what drives you inside, time and time again. He gives us another example that, if he's running on a treadmill and he's running against someone else who's also on a treadmill, he says either he's gonna win, or he's gonna die, on the treadmill.

That amount of command of self is what it takes to bring an idea from just an idea into a real tangible thing. You have to be willing to die for the ideas, concepts and thoughts that you want to be made real in your life. Nothing can be achieved without first mastering yourself. And Will Smith goes on to say that it's not this grand mission that in itself will help you. It is you fixing and changing yourself for that mission.

SELF-DISCIPLINE IS ACTUALLY SELF-LOVE

Another really deep thought on that, that Will Smith continuously brings up, is that self-discipline is actually self-love. In the same way that you love a child. You might love your little cousin, your baby sister; if you see them in a scenario that's not gonna be conducive of their lifestyle, that's not gonna be productive, that's not gonna take them to the next stage, to the next step, that's gonna help them become their higher selves, you would wanna stop them. If you see a small child playing with fire, you would pull them away, because you fear what that fire could do to that child

You fear the pain and suffering that they have to go through, and you have the knowledge to help them. And that, in itself, is love. You're showing love to that person, you're showing love to that other individual, so you have to apply that same kind of love for yourself. You have to apply that same kind of discipline for yourself. That is what Will Smith focuses on. He argues that self-discipline in itself is the self-love, and you have to apply that same kind of discipline and its sternness with that child or a smaller loved one, with yourself. You need to have that same kind of discipline and sternness that you have with them, with yourself.

THERE'S A WAR IN YOUR MIND

ON THIS PAGE, DRAW AND ABSTRACT PICTURE THAT DESCRIBES YOUR STATE OF MIND.

ACTIVITY

BINARY

There's a really cool book that goes into this and I'll go over briefly here. And it goes into an idea that you have two selves inside of you. There's one self that's actively working on the problem at hand, and another self that it's actively remembering everything that's taking in those interactions, in those experiences, not only committing to the Memory, but also formulating plans of what to do next.

That second self informs, tells, dictates, and rules over the first self. The amount of awareness that you have in your second self is the amount of control you have over your first self. That self awareness, that self-discipline is knowing that there's lots of things that are in the world that are gonna try and pull you and control your destiny, control your movements.

SELF-DISCIPLINE IS KNOWING THAT THERE'S LOTS OF THINGS THAT ARE IN THE WORLD THAT ARE GONNA TRY AND PULL YOU AND CONTROL YOUR DESTINY

If you see that pizza, your second self says, "Hey, we don't need that pizza. There's nothing in it for me. I'm on a diet. I feel a little fat, I feel sluggish, I wanna get rid of the cheese and the meat and all the things that I know, intellectually, are causing cancer inside of me."

But, at the same time, you have to pull yourself to the side and say, "Hey, self, you know I love you too much to allow you to do this to yourself and doing it to yourself in a destructive way." Will Smith drives it home, time and time again, that the center of all material successes is self-discipline. Win the war in the mind before you try to win the war outside on the battlefield.

THERE ARE TWO SELVES

That battlefield is being fought every day with your two brains. Nobel prize winner, Daniel Kahneman describes your two brains as follows: there are two selves that have a distinct way in which they move. They have a distinct dichotomy in how these modes of thought move throughout your system. One is Fast and Instinctive. It can help you localize the source of that specific sound. If I say, "war and..." that was your first brain; finishing the sentence "2+2=", that was your first brain

The second system is slower. There's more delay. This is the logical calculated, conscious. It digs into your memory and remembers the exact place where that sound came from. It's the You that figures out what's socially acceptable when you visit your significant other's house. If I ask you to solve 57*36, that's your second brain working. Now, this book goes on to delineate the cognitive biases associated with each of these types of thinking in a very deep way.

NO ONE CAN SAVE YOU

But back on Will Smith. Will Smith goes on to say that if you want to get yourself out of a tough situation, no one can actually pull you out of it. You have to pull yourself out of it, or you'll never get out of the situation in reality. It is your responsibility to love yourself.

It is your responsibility to transmute your fears of not becoming, of not doing the things you hope for, and use that energy to propel yourself forward. Will Smith went as far as to say he's motivated primarily by fear.

IT IS YOUR RESPONSIBILITY TO LOVE YOURSELF.

Right now, he's doing a show on Facebook, where he goes and faces all of his fears. He dives with sharks, he does stand-up in front of his family and Dave Chappelle, he goes sky-diving - you get the idea. And the theory behind that is that fears are so destructive, leading up to the moment right when those fears are not. Being scared of skydiving is actually pointless and useless when you're at home and in the bed. Will Smith gives an example of being 16 hours before you're even at the plane, heart beating, you're in sweats, all of these emotions running through you

. These kinds of emotions can be applied in the same way to people's fears in their lifestyles, for much smaller and simpler things. You can apply the same kind of logic when you're worried about that test paper, when you're worried about how you're gonna do on a performance review, when you're worried about how your boss is gonna feel about what you did. And the actual truth of the fact is that the Law of Attraction says, "You're making it more and more likely that those terrible things will come true."

IF YOU FACE YOUR FEARS, IF YOU ATTACK THEM HEAD-ON, AND YOU OVERCOME THEM, YOU ACTUALLY FREE YOURSELF FROM THE CHAINS OF THOSE FEARS

- WILL SMITH

ON THIS PAGE, WRITE DOWN YOUR FEARS AND A DATE YOU'RE GOING TO FACE THEM.

ACTIVITY

BLISSFUL

Will Smith believes that if you face your fears, if you attack them head-on, and you overcome them, you actually free yourself from the chains of those fears. You will no longer be pulled back by the effects of the things that never happen. Because there's this phenomenon when you ride a roller coaster and you're terrified right up until the point that you're on it, but then, when you're actually in it, it's actually kind of blissful.

the same thing applies to sky-diving. Right up until the point of leaping out of that plane, your heart is beating, you're racing, but in the actual moment when you're overcoming that fear, it is truly life-changing. And it's kind of like those extreme sports and you're not scared right until a thing happens, and then you do it and it's the coolest thing ever.

ATTACK!

The examples could go on. And when it happens, the negative thing, if it even does happen, because sometimes it does, it'll never actually live up to the amount of fear and anxiety you've built inside of yourself in preparation for that moment. And if that happens, all the time that was spent worrying, wondering was wasted; hoping and praying that this thing either would or would not happen.

And all that physical tension that you have, you physically grit your teeth. Your heart physically moves faster. When you perspire, these are physical reactions of that negative emotion being carried through you. And it gets carried with you, into other things that you're doing. And the only way that you can actually get over it is to attack it head-on

"GOD PLACED THE BEST THINGS IN LIFE ON THE OTHER SIDE OF TERROR."

There's a great quote that he pulls in, and he says, "God placed the best things in life on the other side of terror." And what that means is you can't actually get those things you want without going through those fears. There's this assumption that you can somehow out-think and out manipulate your way to bypass and skip over the things you have to do, in order to get what you want. That you can somehow avoid the taxation that life has on the things you're requesting of it.

But unfortunately, because of the immutable laws of nature, that is simply impossible. Everything you desire requires some tax. And I don't necessarily mean a monetary tax, but sometimes that's what it is. And you might say, "Oh, but the rich get richer and it isn't fair. Every single opportunity is this and that was placed before them and...". It's all relative to your own life.

IT'S ALL RELATIVE TO YOUR OWN LIFE.

And what I mean by that is, if you grow with millions of dollars, you probably don't have the same kind of appreciation that you would if you actually earned that million dollars. The value in things that you want is the value when you achieve it. It serves your own ego. It serves your self-identity. When they come into fruition, you personally, inside, value it at a value that cannot be replicated.

It can't come from the outside. You can look online, you can look at Forbes, you can look at all of your favorite rappers and celebrities and try to pick out the things that you think make them happy, that you think make them who they are. And you can try to extrapolate all those things and if you could just accomplish and get that thing, then you would be happy as a person. But if those goals are yours, that's fine. But you have to understand that none of those things will matter if you get them without paying the price that it comes. And the price that comes with it, is discipline.

THE PRICE FOR SUCCESS IS DISCIPLINE

YOU HAVE
TO DECIDE

You have to decide, internally, that even if you get the wins that other people think are successful, that other people say are amazing, super-incredible, that if it doesn't come from inside of you, you're not going to get the effects you're looking for. You're not going to get what you think you see other people who are super successful and super-rich, getting out of it.

They are those same people who are super successful and super-rich, and some of them commit suicide, because the internal clock, the internal motor that is inside of you, driving you, has to be what determines your next steps. Because if not, if you are taking these other steps to fulfill other people's desires for yourself, you won't get what you're seeking for.

TO DETERMINE YOUR OWN SELF WORTH BY OTHER PEOPLE'S OPINIONS, IS LIKE LOOKING IN A BROKEN MIRROR AND JUDGING YOURSELF ON HOW YOU LOOK IN THAT BROKEN MIRROR

- WILL SMITH

NO BROKEN MIRRORS

Will Smith goes on to make another key point, and that is, "To determine your own self worth by other people's opinions, is like looking in a broken mirror and judging yourself on how you look in that broken mirror." And that's deep and impactful because other people, by nature of being other people, can only have an outside perspective on who you are.

It is impossible and illogical to think that another person can understand, can feel, can have the context of everything that has happened in your life, every accomplishment, every failure, every testament. How can another individual have all of that information about yourself?

HOW CAN ANOTHER INDIVIDUAL HAVE ALL OF THAT INFORMATION ABOUT YOURSELF?

then you expect them to form an opinion on you and give it back to you, even if that person lived with you their entire life, they can't have access to the inner workings of who you are, by nature of looking at you, by nature of being next to you.

It is impossible. If you're looking into a broken mirror, you are looking at a false reflection of who you are, so that's why it's very important for you to know who you are. If you don't know who you are, then you can't know yourself enough to know what kind of person you can become.

KNOW THYSELF

The Greek saying, "Know thyself" was inscribed in the temple of Apollo at Delphi. This phrase was later extrapolated by Socrates, who said that "an unexamined life is not even a life worth living." And what that means is, if you don't take the time to constantly look back and analyze your own choices, analyze your own mistakes, steps, and things that you've done to make yourself who you are, you can't become a better person

You're kind of wasting your time with this whole life experience, because humanity is one of the only species that have self-awareness. This fact makes you unique. The fact that you can watch yourself from outside of yourself, is what makes you uniquely human. It is what makes you a creature unlike anything else in this Universe.

LOVE ALL
OF THE
ASPECTS
OF YOU

ON THIS PAGE, WRITE DOWN EVERYTHING YOU LOVE ABOUT YOURSELF.

ACTIVITY

WATCH WHO YOU REALLY ARE

So, if you can know yourself and that uniqueness is your self-discipline and that self-discipline is the act of loving the person that you're getting to know, it is the act of loving all of the aspects of that person that you are. You have to take yourself out of yourself and watch who you really are, and give yourself the time to show yourself who you are. Just like dating any other person or any other situation, you wanna get to know who that person is, first. You wanna know the basics:

Where they're from? What are they into? But eventually, if you stick around that person just long enough, you'll start to dive deep. You'll start to see what motivate that person. You'll start to see what kind of things draw that person to action. You'll start to see what kind of flaws that person may have, things that annoy you, things you love about them

DISCRETION

The object of being self-aware is that you can use that same kind of discretion that you would use with a stranger, someone you just met, in a romantic sense, you can apply that same kind of discretion with yourself.

When you start to get to know yourself, in the same way that you would treat that loved one, or that romantic passion, you can convert that love and that same energy into falling in love with yourself.

IT ISN'T GONNA BE RIGHT ALL THE TIME

And just like when you're falling in love with someone else, it isn't gonna be right all the time, you're not gonna like the things that your other self is doing, but that's no reason to "kick them in the balls", metaphorically. You have to love them, discipline them into being the person and the space that they can become.

You have to be able to tell yourself, "Hey, I know you're in this place right now, and that's not exactly where you want to be, and I know you're not doing all the things that you could do, that you want to do. But here's a small step you can take, and we can change that right now."

THE WORLD HAS PLANS

That's what people like Will Smith know. And that's what people like Will Smith do. It takes good, talented people and makes them become impactful and legendary. It's what breaks through the borderline of what could be, and what can become.

It's the other side of the things you're looking to accomplish, because the entire world, all of the energy that's floating around out there, has its own plans for what it wants you to go out and do. It has its own plans of what direction it wants you to go in.

THE HAVE DIRECTIVES FOR YOUR ENERGY

And usually, it's wherever is most beneficial to that other energy, be that your mother, your father, your brother or your sister, the police, that teacher, your boss. They all have directives for your life.

They all have directives for your energy and how they want to see it used. And it can affect how you feel about yourself. When you start to measure yourself by how well you're conforming to all of the ideas of everyone else and what they want, you take out all of this different energies and you put them in a filter.

DETERMINE FOR YOURSELF WHAT ARE YOUR GOALS

ON THIS PAGE, WRITE DOWN YOUR GOAL AND A DATE YOU'RE GOING ACHIEVE THEM BY.

ACTIVITY

I'M TAKING CONTROL

Actually determine for yourself what are your goals, what do you truly, deeply, down in your soul, when no one else is watching, when Instagram is down, when Facebook is down, when you're in that room by yourself, with the lights off, what kinds of things motivate you? What kinds of things get you going? What kind of things push you to be different, to be better?

What kind of things make you feel like you're truly finding who you are? Once you find those things, once you know where you're going, and how you wanna get there, the only step is discipline and love in yourself. And those two things will catapult you into doing all of these things to prove your love for yourself. You say, "Self, this is what we're doing, and I'm taking control of the reins. Because if I don't, we'll never get there. We'll never see our potential fulfilled."

IT SOUNDS WEIRD TO REFER TO YOURSELF IN MULTIPLE PEOPLE, BUT THAT'S REALLY WHO YOU ARE. THE CHRISTIANS CALL IT, "THE SOUL AND THE FLESH." EVERY MAJOR RELIGION HAS SOME KIND OF REPRESENTATION FOR THIS WARRING DUO THAT'S GOING INSIDE OF YOU.

SKILL > TALENT

But back to Will Smith. One thing that has always fascinated me, with about the way that Will Smith thinks, is he had the audacity to say, "I've never seen myself as very talented."

Yeah, this is the same guy. Will Smith from your favorite sitcom, from your favorite movie, from maybe your favorite summertime song. The same Will Smith said he never saw himself as very talented.

TALENT WILL FAIL YOU

And he goes on to say, that talent is going to fail you if you're not skilled, and that most people confuse talent and skill. Talent, you're born with; skill is only developed after painstaking, grueling hours, and hours, and hours, and hours, and hours of failure.

That is the only way you receive mastery. And if you don't achieve your skills, if you don't rein yourself in to go get those skills, you'll never be able to communicate with your artistry.

WILL'S FATHER

Will Smith's dad did something that was unbelievable to me. He had this shop with a brick wall in front, and his father actually tore down the brick wall. Tore it down, physically, real-life tore down the brick wall in the front of the store. he brought over Will, and his brother. At the time, they were 12 and 9, and he told them, "Build the wall!" He told a 12-year-old and a 9-year-old, "You see that wall, that I just broke? Build it!" And at first, their response was, "I can't do that. I'm 9, I can't build this wall." He said, "Build the wall." And months go by, months go by, months go by, a year goes by, and eventually, they built that wall

Will Smith said he pulled out of that lesson, was that you don't go into it looking, "We're gonna build the biggest wall ever!" You go into it with, "I'm going to lay this brick in the absolute most perfect, unmistakably, mastered brick lay of this one brick." And you're gonna do that once, and then you're gonna do it again, and again, and again, and eventually, you've got this wall, the wall you didn't think you could do. That even your mind couldn't allow you to believe you could achieve. You just have to take the first step.

IT'S HARD!

RESPONSIBILITY

And it's so hard! I know, it's hard, because you have these two selves in you, warring. And you have to take the reins and pull it in the right direction.

This is not only important for you and for yourself, but this is important for everyone around you, everyone you come in contact with, everyone that you ever meet, interact with, have sex with.

YOU MIGHT NOT BE ABLE TO MAKE THEM HAPPY, BUT YOUR PRESENCE CAN MAKE THEM BETTER.

You will be having an impact on their life. And Will Smith's grandmother said, "You have a spiritual responsibility to make every group you come in contact with, better." A spiritual responsibility.

You might not be able to make them happy, but your presence can make them better. If you're not making someone else's life better, you're wasting your time. Will Smith says, "Your life only becomes better by making other people's lives better."

FOR WILL SMITH, HE SAYS HE WANTS TO REPRESENT AN IDEA, TO REPRESENT POSSIBILITY, TO REPRESENT THE IDEA THAT YOU REALLY CAN MAKE THIS LIFE ANYTHING YOU WANT.

PRESIDENTIAL WILL

right after Will Smith overcame one of his greatest fears, stand-up comedy - you should go check it out, it's hilarious - right after he did that, a paparazzi came up to the car with him and Dave Chapelle inside, and they asked Will Smith if he's gonna run for President. He said, "You know what? Because you said that, I'll consider it!" And

Dave Chappelle said he would be vice-president. Personally, I'm all here for it. 100% here for the Will Smith - Dave Chappelle ticket. But what was important about that, and what I saw at that moment, was that Will Smith was kind of serious. And there's other interviews that he's had, where he extrapolates upon the idea of becoming the President of the United States, and that he's considered it. It's not ruled out.

"THERE'S NO REASON TO HAVE A PLAN B BECAUSE IT DISTRACTS FROM PLAN A."

ON THIS PAGE, WRITE DOWN YOUR IMMEDIATE PLANS AND WHO YOU NEED TO MAKE THEM HAPPEN.

TRUST

Will Smith said, "There's no reason to have a plan B because it distracts from plan A." You have to trust in the immutable laws of nature, or as some have called, "Infinite Intelligence",

Trust that as soon as you walk out into the world, declare what is going to happen and start subconsciously second selfly becoming the person that would walk that path, the Universe will start to move in your favor.

THE IDEAS IN YOUR HEAD ARE ALIVE

The ideas in your head are alive. And if you feed them, they will grow. And if you share them, they will spread. And if you remind that person that you shared it with, they'll grow inside of their head.

These thoughts serve as magnets and beacons to the Universe to pull it in the direction that you wanted to go, the direction that you wanted to be.

HE WHO SAYS HE CAN, AND HE WHO SAYS HE CAN'T, ARE BOTH USUALLY RIGHT.

One of Will's favorite quotes is "He who says he can, and he who says he can't, are both usually right." And that quote means that if you think yourself into failure, you will probably fail. If you think yourself into success, you will probably succeed.

This is the evidence of manifestation. This is the evidence of those magnets, of those beacons that you put out into the world. And they become energized through your emotions. Your physical response to those ideas in the world.

IF YOU HAVE A DREAM, YOU'VE GOT TO PROTECT IT

YOU MUST RETIRE

If you have a dream, you've got to protect it, and if you want something in the world, you have to pull it to you. And that's also why you can't make another person happy.

Will Smith brought this up in a conversation he had with Jada Pinkett, and he said that he retired from trying to make her happy.

THE IDEAS IN YOUR HEAD ARE ALIVE

At first it sounds a bit harsh, but in reality, what it means is that you, as an individual, shouldn't come to relationships of any kind with an empty cup, and expect the other person to fill you up

if you both have an empty cup, neither one of you can fill each other. However, if you come to it already happy and full, and you recognize that that other person's happiness is actually out of your control.

HAPPINESS CAN ONLY COME FROM YOUR INTERNAL COMPASS AND ACCOMPLISHMENTS. IT CAN ONLY COME FROM THE GOALS THAT YOU SET AND THAT YOU MAKE FOR YOURSELF

FILL YOUR OWN CUP FIRST

That applies to anyone else, as well. And two people can choose to walk together and still be themselves and the act of the walk is shared, but they are still themselves, because if you start to look for other people to always fill your cup, it's a recipe for you to be let down.

in the worst cases, it can be destructive to who you are. And you taking responsibility for making sure your cup is full, is actually an act of emotional self-defense. It's actually a protective barrier you're placing around the "we" that is inside of you

EMOTIONAL DEFENCE

In the worst cases, it can be destructive to who you are. And you taking responsibility for making sure your cup is full, is actually an act of emotional self-defense. It's actually a protective barrier you're placing around the "we" that is inside of you

It is you taking back the power of guiding your own life towards your own goals, which is the only way you can find your happiness. Failure in doing that is a part of the mastery of self.

FAILURE IS NECESSARY

It's another key point that Will Smith always tries to drive, "Failure is necessary." It's a massive part of becoming successful. You can't be successful without failure. Working out is a controlled failure.

You wanna take your muscles to the absolute limit, 'till they rip because that is where the growth is. And if you're afraid to take yourself just like you're afraid to take your muscles to that point of ripping, then you'll never get the gains.

"I THINK I CAN BEAT MIKE TYSON"

BETTER TO GET HIT IN THE FACE AND THEN RUN, THAN TO NEVER STEP IN THE RING IN THE FIRST PLACE

Will Smith once wrote a song called, "I think I can beat Mike Tyson". And in it, he said, "A good run is better than a bad stand any day." And what he was saying was, in the song, he decided to fight Mike Tyson. THE Mike Tyson

And he hyped it up, he brought everyone there, and then, as Mike always says, "Everyone's got a plan, 'till they get hit in the face." But Will Smith's retort is that is better to get hit in the face and then run than to never step in the ring in the first place, even if it's Mike Tyson throwing the punches.

ON THIS PAGE, WRITE A LETTER TO YOUR
FUTURE SELF AND COMPLIMENT
YOURSELF ON ALL THE THINGS
YOU KNOW YOU'LL ACCOMPLISH.

ACTIVITY